STAY

THE TRUE STORY OF TEN DOGS

By Michaela Muntean

Photographs by K. C. Bailey and Stephen Kazmierski

SCHOLASTIC PRESS / NEW YORK

For beloved dogs, past and present—Trouble, Strife, Jones, Tatum, Beau, and Tess. But above all, for Flynn. —MM

To homeless dogs everywhere—we see you. —KCB & SK

For my family, those of you with two legs and those with four. You are my soul mates. —LA

Our most sincere thanks to the Big Apple Circus for their generosity in allowing us to photograph on their grounds. We also wish to acknowledge their over thirty years of commitment to excellence in the sensitive handling, care, and training of their animal partners while providing the joys of classical circus to thousands of appreciative audiences.

Library of Congress Cataloging-in-Publication Data
Muntean, Michaela.
Stay: the true story of ten dogs / by Michaela Muntean ; photographs by K. C. Bailey and Stephen Kazmierski. — 1st ed.   p. cm.
1. Dog adoption — Juvenile literature. 2. Anastasini, Luciano — Juvenile literature. 3. Circus performers — Juvenile literature. 4. Dogs — Behavior — Juvenile literature. I. Bailey, K. C. II. Kazmierski, Stephen. III. Title.
SF427.M86 2012   636.7'0887 — dc22   2010050064   ISBN 978-0-545-23497-9

10 9 8 7 6 5 4 3 2 1   12 13 14 15 16
Printed in Singapore 46
First edition, April 2012
The text was set in Bookman Old Style and the display type was set in Chinchilla Dots.
Book design by Charles Kreloff

INTRODUCTION

When I was three years old, I went to the circus with my mother and watched a very small car disgorge an impossible number of clowns. This trick, this stupefying display of possibility and plenty, made a profound impact on me. It convinced me that the most common object could contain wonders beyond all my imagining, and that things are not always as they seem.

We, too, are not always as we seem. Our best selves are sometimes hidden. But what if someone saw us, truly saw us, and believed in the wonders waiting inside of us?

This is the story of Luciano Anastasini and his pound dogs. It is a story of second chances, belief, and love. Mostly, though, it is a story of the miracles that can occur when we (dog or human) are extended the grace of being well and truly seen by another.

We are grumpy, scruffy, restless, broken. We have done things we wish we hadn't done. But inside each of us, there waits an infinity of dazzle, color, humor, hope, sadness, joy . . . an endless parade of clowns.

We just need someone to open the door, to see us. And to believe.

—KATE DiCAMILLO
author of *Because of Winn-Dixie*

SOMETIMES A DOG

will show up when a person needs one most.

SOMETIMES A PERSON

will show up when a dog needs one most.

SOMETIMES A DOG AND A PERSON

will find each other at just the right moment—a moment when they need each other more than either could ever imagine.

THIS IS THE TRUE STORY

of one man and ten dogs. They were fortunate enough to find one another, but luck alone does not turn around lives.

Luciano Anastasini's entire family—his parents, his grand-parents, all the way back to his great-great-great-great-grandparents—were circus performers, and he became one, too. By the time he was twelve, he was a famous juggler and acrobat.

Luciano loved the circus. He loved the glitter and flash, the wonder and awe. Nothing could compare to the edge-of-seat tension as trapeze artists flew through the air or tightrope walkers danced across the wire. It was the only life Luciano knew. It was the life he'd been born for.

And so it was until that day in Chicago, when he fell fifty feet from the high wire. He broke so many bones, it took four operations to put him back together. The doctors told him he would eventually heal, but his days as an acrobat—or of doing any kind of fancy stunt—were over.

Luciano, 10, his little brother, Giovanni, and their dog, Pepe

Luciano's father, Renato, helps him learn to do a flip

But the circus was Luciano's home, and he wanted to stay. He sold tickets. He put up posters. He dreamed of the day he'd once again have an act of his own. Slowly, an idea began to take shape in his mind.

In the act he imagined, he would need partners—furry, four-legged partners.

Of course, he could have found dogs through a breeder. Or at a pet store. But if his idea worked, Luciano would be getting a second chance. Perhaps he could give some dogs a second chance, too. So Luciano went looking for the ones no one wanted.

BOWSER

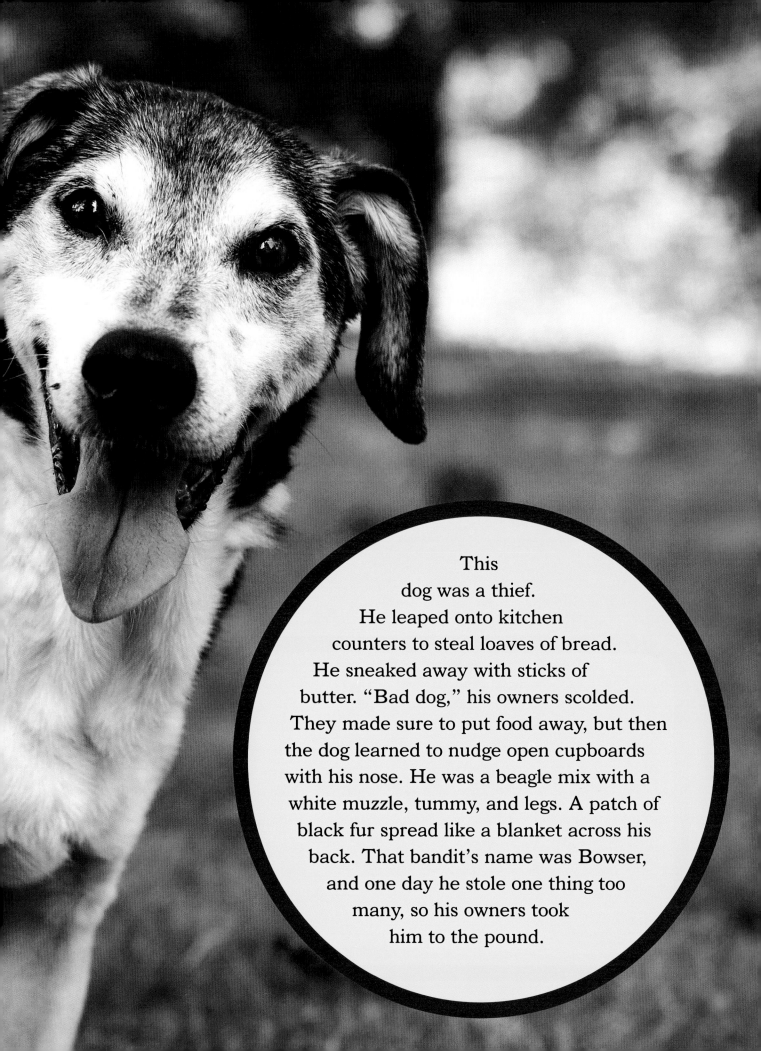

This
dog was a thief.
He leaped onto kitchen
counters to steal loaves of bread.
He sneaked away with sticks of
butter. "Bad dog," his owners scolded.
They made sure to put food away, but then
the dog learned to nudge open cupboards
with his nose. He was a beagle mix with a
white muzzle, tummy, and legs. A patch of
black fur spread like a blanket across his
back. That bandit's name was Bowser,
and one day he stole one thing too
many, so his owners took
him to the pound.

PENNY

She was adorable. Everyone agreed that the little bichon frise with the easy smile and the cloud of white fur was hard to resist. Three times, Penny was adopted from the shelter; three times, she was returned. People handed her back with the same sad sigh and complaint: The dog spun around madly in circles. She ran into walls and furniture. Was she blind? No, it seemed she could see. Maybe she was crazy. She certainly drove the people who took her home crazy with her weird behavior. Whatever the reason for it, Penny now had three strikes against her.

A restaurant owner called the police. There was a stray that kept coming around, tipping over garbage cans and scrounging for scraps. The animal control unit tracked down the terrier, who was so thin, his ribs poked out like bicycle spokes. The dog had three white legs and one black one, which the people at the shelter thought looked like a stick. So that's what they named him.

STICK

TYKE

Tyke was a schnauzer with a bad attitude. He wouldn't do anything anyone asked. In fact, he usually did the opposite. Told to stay, he ran. Asked to sit, he jumped. Perhaps it was because he didn't feel well—he had a nasty skin condition that had gone untreated—or maybe he was just a crabby guy. Then, one day, he bit someone.

They named her Cocoa because she was a Dalmatian with chocolate-colored spots rather than black ones. The people she lived with didn't mind her running and jumping, but they did mind her digging. Cocoa tore up grass and flower beds. She pawed so many holes in the lawn, it looked like a minefield. The holes got deeper and her owners' patience got thinner, until they decided Cocoa had to go.

COCOA

Luciano didn't care that Bowser was a thief. It didn't matter that Cocoa liked to dig or that Tyke was a grouch. When he looked at Stick, he saw an intelligent dog—a dog he'd like to get to know. As for Penny, well . . . if anyone had ever looked directly into her eyes the way Luciano did, they would have seen that she was neither blind nor crazy, but cross-eyed, and that didn't bother him, either.

"No one's perfect," Luciano told the dogs, and he took all five of them home to the circus.

The only problem was, Luciano wasn't a dog trainer. He didn't believe in teaching a dog to do something it wouldn't do on its own, such as walk on its front legs or do a backflip. What he did believe in was letting a dog be a dog.

The best way to do that, he decided, was to let them show him what *they* wanted to do. Then, somehow, he'd figure out a way to let them do it.

As the dogs ran and played together, Luciano paid special attention to each of them.

While Bowser's previous owners had seen a sneak and a thief, Luciano saw a clever dog with a good sense of balance.

Cocoa wouldn't stop digging. As Luciano filled in the holes she made, he thought about why she did it. He suspected she had so much energy, she didn't know what to do with herself. Digging was her way of staying busy.

Stick was quick on his feet and enjoyed strutting about on his back legs. "Shall we dance?" Luciano would ask him, and they'd waltz around the circus grounds together.

Penny was a gentle, sweet-natured dog, but Luciano couldn't keep her from crashing into things. Finally, he tried making himself cross-eyed. If he could see the world the way she saw it, maybe he could help her.

"Poor Penny," Luciano said with his eyes crossed. "No wonder you're confused—you see two of everything!"

He figured out that Penny always headed for what she saw directly in front of her, but the actual object—an open door, for example—was at least four inches to the left of where she saw it. So instead of running through the open space, she usually slammed into the door frame.

Perhaps everything depended on how you looked at it. Where others had seen headaches and problems, Luciano saw hope and possibilities. Over time, he believed he could help Bowser, Cocoa, Stick, and Penny become the dogs they were meant to be.

And then there was Tyke.

His skin problem had cleared up, but it hadn't made him any easier to get along with. Everyone told Luciano he should give up on that rotten-tempered schnauzer, but Luciano wouldn't do it. He was determined to find a way to get through to Tyke.

One day, he stuffed his pockets with Tyke's favorite treats. "Hello, Tyke," he said softly. Tyke snarled. "Good boy," said Luciano. Tyke growled and snapped. Luciano praised him and gave him a treat. No matter how terrible Tyke acted, he was told he was a good dog. Eventually, he sat quietly and looked up at Luciano, completely baffled.

Luciano knew it was a crazy thing to do. No one with a lick of sense would reward a dog for bad behavior. But Tyke was a special case. He was so contrary, he did everything backward; maybe he even *thought* backward. So Luciano tried thinking backward, too, and it worked.

After many weeks together, there came a day when Luciano felt he and the dogs knew and trusted one another. This would be important, because they were going to be partners.

For nearly two years, they worked together. It was fun. It was hard. It was worth it, because in the end, Luciano found a way for all of the dogs to do what they did best.

Bowser, with his fantastic sense of balance, leaped onto a barrel, rolling and riding around the ring.

Luciano used a leash to guide Penny onto a bench, over a hurdle, or through a hoop, until she eventually learned which was the true image of the two she always saw. From then on, that cross-eyed dog never missed her mark.

Cocoa did seem to have endless energy, and Luciano let her use it. She was a strong and agile athlete who easily jumped flags and hurdles. She was also incredibly fast, and could run the outer ring at dizzying speed.

All the dogs liked scampering up ladders and scooting down slides, but it was Tyke who made the trick funny. When he got to the top of a slide, he turned around and slid down backward. Typical Tyke. Soon, some of the other dogs tried sliding backward, too.

Amid the leaping, dashing dogs was Luciano himself. He'd taught Cocoa to knock him over; Bowser would then roll him up in a carpet by nudging it with his nose. Stick jumped into his arms; Penny flew over his back. It was a funny, fast-paced act. Luciano wanted audiences to laugh at him and his clever dogs.

But what would happen when there *was* an audience? So far, they'd only performed for a tent full of empty seats. When those seats were filled with shouting, laughing people, when lights flashed and music blared, would the dogs be distracted or, worse, frightened?

It was time to find out.

Luciano asked the principal of a local elementary school if he and his dogs could give a show for the students.

It was a day Luciano will never forget. He'd been in the circus his entire life, and he'd never once been nervous before a performance. Now his heart was thumping. But when he looked at the dogs' faces, he relaxed. They weren't worried; why should he be?

He took a deep breath and walked into the school gym, the dogs trotting behind him. The room was packed with children sitting on the floor in a big circle. The first thing the dogs did was race into the crowd. They just wanted to say hello to the kids, who jumped up, eager to play.

Soon everyone was running around, squealing and laughing. It was chaos. The kids loved it, but all Luciano could think was *uh-oh*. Fortunately, the principal asked him if that was part of the act. Quickly, Luciano said yes, called the dogs back, and started their routine.

Penny, Bowser, Cocoa, Tyke, and Stick darted and danced. They bounded through hoops and vaulted over hurdles. They were a whirl of fur—of paws and tails and ears—and the kids went wild. The dogs felt it, too. They loved the energy, the charge of being in the spotlight. At that moment, Luciano knew they'd become performers.

They were ready for the Big Top.

Soon, Luciano Anastasini and his Pound Puppies were stars. They were hired by the biggest circuses in the business, and they crisscrossed the country, performing in show after show.

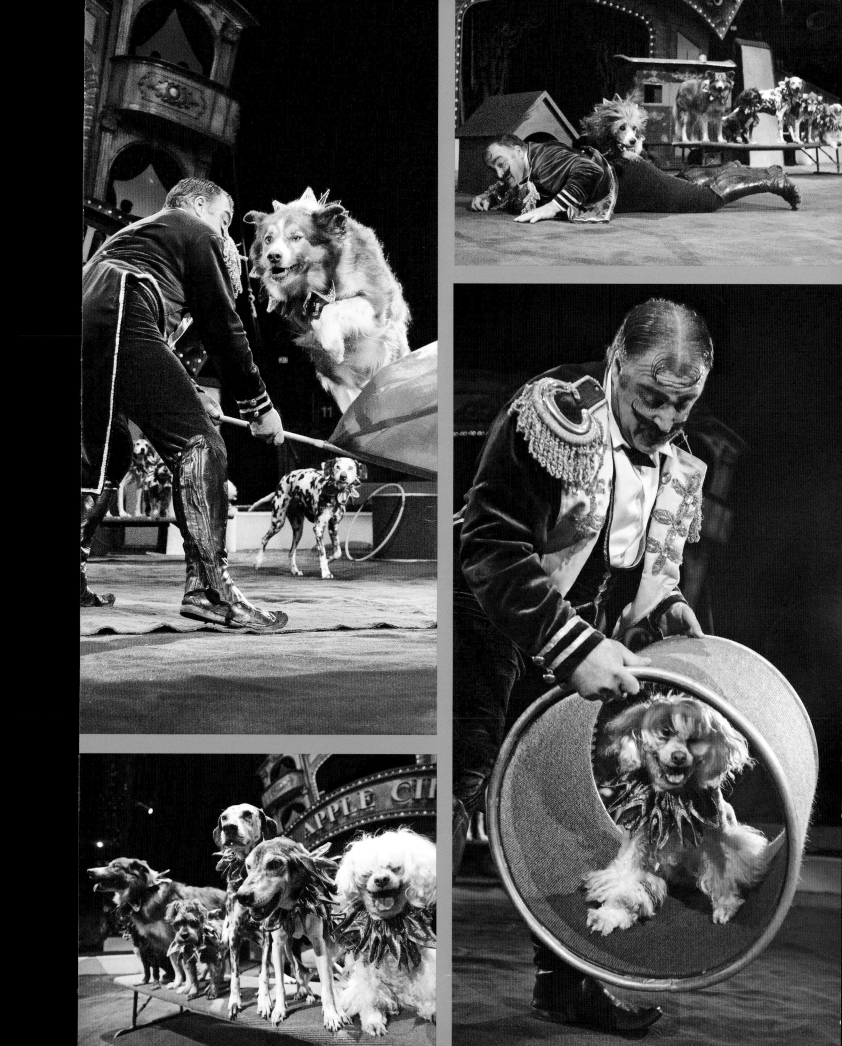

Word spread about the circus man who took in hopeless-case dogs. People even began bringing him dogs they'd given up on, dogs like E-Z, whose owners said they couldn't him keep from running away.

Luciano solved the problem by clipping a leash to E-Z's collar and fastening the other end to his belt. All day long, E-Z was by his side, and Luciano would talk to him. By the end of a month, E-Z must have decided he wanted to stay, because he never ran away again. Luciano says E-Z is now the most dependable dog he's ever known, and could probably run the act by himself!

With so many dogs, Luciano now has a huge trailer where each dog has its own area, bed, and blanket. The trailer is heated in winter and air-conditioned in summer. There is a television set and a radio to keep the dogs occupied. The trailer is always parked beside Luciano's mobile home. When the circus is ready to move on, he connects the dogs' trailer to his and they set out for the next city.

On their days off, Luciano gives the dogs a bath. He brushes and grooms them. They go for walks, or just hang out together. Luciano knows that life can't always be a circus, and sometimes they need to do nothing at all. He also tries to spend time alone with each dog. He says that dogs aren't that hard to understand. It's true that they all need love and attention, but they also need someone who thinks they're special. Of course, everyone needs that, whether they're a dog or not.

New dogs have joined the act. Wherever Luciano goes, there's always a dog that needs a home, and he rescues the ones that he can. Just as he's always done, he patiently gets to know each one to discover what that dog likes to do. The only difference now is that the new ones learn from the older ones. Many times, they copy what they see the other dogs do. Some are so eager to join in, it's as if they're saying, "Get out of the way, let me try—look, I can do it!"

MEEMO

That's the way it was with Meemo, a Border collie mix. After only a few months, he was ready to join the act.

FREE

Free, a poodle mix, lives up to his name. He's free-spirited and easygoing. Nothing ever seems to bother him.

SAMMY

Sammy, a small black-and-white terrier, took longer. He's a nervous little guy, but very hardworking. Luciano's trying to get him to relax and enjoy himself more.

ROWDY

Then there's Rowdy, the newest member of the group. His owner said he was unmanageable and asked Luciano to take him. He's a beautiful dog, full of spirit and energy, and Luciano thinks he's going to be a star.

People frequently say to Luciano, "You saved those dogs." To that, Luciano shrugs and says maybe that's true, maybe it's not. What he knows for certain is this: They saved him.

After his accident, they helped him put his life back together, and he is grateful to each and every one of them. Dogs don't care about yesterday; they don't worry about tomorrow. They live for now—*right* now, and Luciano tries to do the same.

"We are lucky, my dogs and me," he says. "We have a job we love, a job that makes people smile. But most of all, we have each other."

A LETTER FROM LUCIANO

There is something you should know about me: I smell like a dog. No, that's not true—I smell like *ten* dogs! When I meet a new dog, I can see the confusion in its eyes; I can feel it wondering, *What kind of creature* are *you?*

I hope I'm the kind of creature that that dog will want to get to know, because I love dogs. I love living with them and working with them.

The most important thing to remember when teaching a dog anything, whether it's to sit or to jump through a hoop, is to be kind, consistent, and patient. I use only positive reinforcement, lots of treats, and lots of praise. Dogs, by nature, are happy animals, and you should never do anything that would break a dog's spirit.

There was a time when nearly all dogs had jobs. Most were bred to herd, to hunt, to guard. These days, there aren't many jobs for dogs, and dogs need to be busy. They like to have something to think about, and they like to have fun. Oftentimes, when dogs misbehave, I think it's just because they're bored.

If you have a dog, go spend some time playing with it right now . . . and please say hello to that dog from me.

Your friend,

Luciano D. L.